SRA Open Court Reading

Light and Sound

Grade 1

McGraw Hill Education

Program Authors

Carl Bereiter, Ph.D.
Andrew Biemiller, Ph.D.
Joe Campione, Ph.D.
Doug Fuchs, Ph.D.
Lynn Fuchs, Ph.D.
Steve Graham, Ph.D.
Karen Harris, Ph.D.
Jan Hirshberg, Ed.D.
Anne McKeough, Ph.D.
Marsha Roit, Ed.D.
Marlene Scardamalia, Ph.D.
Marcy Stein, Ph.D.
Gerald H. Treadway Jr, Ph.D.

Photo Credits

4 TommyBrison/Shutterstock; **5** rozbyshaka/iStock/Getty Images Plus, Jodie Griggs/Moment Open/Getty Images, ©KidStock/Blend Images LLC; **30** Steve Satushek/Stockbyte/Getty Images; **31-39** John Carleton/Getty Images, somchaisom/iStockphoto/Getty Images; **56** Blue Jean Images/Alamy Images; **57** DCPhoto/Alamy. **Back Cover:** rozbyshaka/iStock/Getty Images Plus, Jodie Griggs/Moment Open/Getty Images, ©KidStock/Blend Images LLC.

Acknowledgments

Grateful acknowledgment is given to the following publishers and copyright owners for permissions granted to reprint selections from their publications. All possible care has been taken to trace ownership and secure permission for each selection included. In case of any errors or omissions, the Publisher will be pleased to make suitable acknowledgments in future editions.

Me and My Shadow; Click Magazine, May 2014. Copyright © by Carus Publishing Company. Reproduced with permission. All Cricket Media material is copyrighted by Carus Publishing Company, d/b/a Cricket Media, and/or various authors and illustrators. Any commercial use or distribution of material without permission is strictly prohibited. Please visit http://www.cricketmedia.com/info/licensing2 for licensing and http://www.cricketmedia.com for subscriptions.

"The Sun" by Gareth Lancaster. Used by permission of the author. All rights reserved.

"The Star" by Jane Taylor.

MHEonline.com

McGraw Hill Education

Send all inquiries to:
McGraw-Hill Education
8787 Orion Place
Columbus, OH 43240

ISBN: 978-0-07-669118-0
MHID: 0-07-669118-7

Printed in the United States of America.

7 8 9 MER 25 24 23

UNIT 4

Light and Sound

Book 1

Table of Contents

UNIT
4 Light and Sound

Theme Connections

What would you see or hear in these images?

Background Builder Video

connected.mcgraw-hill.com

Essential Questions Where have you seen a shadow? When do you see your shadow?

Me and My Shadow

by Amy Tao
illustrated by Virginia Allyn

Go outside on a sunny morning and find your shadow. How long is it? Which way does it point?

When you face your shadow, where is the sun?

If you turn so your shadow is to the side, where is the sun?

Now face the sun, but don't look directly at it. Where is your shadow?

Never look right at the sun. You could hurt your eyes.

Are your shadow and the sun ever on the same side of you?

Your shadow is always on the side of you that is away from the sun.

That's because to make a shadow, you need light, something that blocks the light, and a place for the shadow to land. The light, the light blocker, and the shadow always line up in a straight path in the same order.

Do you feel cooler when you stand in the shadow of a tree or building?

The tree and building are blocking the sun's light and heat, so their shadows stay cool.

You can use a flashlight or lamp instead of sunlight to make shadows. And if you use your hands to block the light in just the right way, you can even make some amazing shadow animals.

At lunchtime, go outside again and stand in the same place you stood in the morning. Find your shadow.

How long is your shadow? Which way does it point? Where is the sun?

Look again in the late afternoon.
Has your shadow changed direction?
Where is the sun?

You should find that your shadow is shortest around noon, when the sun is high above your head. It is longest just before sunset, when the sun appears low in the sky.

And the direction it points in the afternoon is different from the one it points to in the morning.

You stood in the same place each time, so why did your shadow move and change size?

Because the sun's light shone from a different direction at different times of the day. If you drew a picture of where the sun appeared every hour, it would look something like this.

But is the sun really moving?
No, it is Earth that is moving.

Earth is shaped like a giant ball and spins like a top.

We don't feel any movement because Earth spins so smoothly and everything on Earth moves together with us. It's a little like when you ride in a car.

While the car travels at a constant speed, without slowing down or speeding up, you might not feel the car's motion. Instead, all the buildings and trees outside the car look like they are moving.

It takes 24 hours—one whole day and night—for Earth to make one complete spin.

When the side of Earth where you live faces the sun, you have daylight. But the other side of the world is in shadow then. It is night there.

As Earth spins, your part of the world turns away from the sun. The other side of Earth faces the sun and blocks the sun from reaching you. Now you're in the shadow, and it is night.

At night everything outside is in shadow. But during the day, you can learn a lot from looking at shadows.

Essential Questions How does the movement of the sun affect our day? Why don't we always see the sun?

The Sun

by Gareth Lancaster
illustrated by Ilana Exelby

Don't you think the sun is bright?
I wonder where it goes at night?
Does it sleep or does it hide?
Or is the moon its other side?

Does it hide behind the hills?
Late at night as outside chills?
Do you think it needs to rest?
From all that warming it does best?

Could it even have a home?
Maybe in London or even in Rome?
Or does it just float around?
Moving slowly from town to town?

Yes, I think it must do that!
After all the earth's not flat.
So the sun goes round and round
Spreading sunshine on the ground!

Essential Questions How are stars similar to the sun? How are they different?

The Star

by Jane Taylor
illustrated by Ilana Exelby

Twinkle, twinkle, little star,
How I wonder what you are!
Up above the world so high,
Like a diamond in the sky.

When the blazing sun is gone,
When he nothing shines upon,
Then you show your little light,
Twinkle, twinkle, all the night.

Then the traveler in the dark,
Thanks you for your tiny spark,
He could not see which way to go,
If you did not twinkle so.

In the dark blue sky you keep,
And often through my curtains peep,
For you never shut your eye,
Till the sun is in the sky.

As your bright and tiny spark,
Lights the traveler in the dark,
Though I know not what you are,
Twinkle, twinkle, little star.

Essential Questions When do you see the moon? Is it always in the same place?

Watching the Moon

by Abi Manickam

In school today I learned that moonlight does not come from the moon. Moonlight comes from the sun shining on the moon.

I decided to look at the moon every night for one month and write down what I saw in a journal.

Day 1

The moon is so big and bright tonight. I can easily see the trees outside. The position of the moon is high in the sky. This is called the full moon.

Day 5

Tonight the moon looks like it is getting smaller. But it is not getting smaller. I just see less sunlight on the moon.

Day 8

The moon's shape seems to be changing. I see only half of the moon now. The rest of it is in a shadow.

Day 10

The moon continues to look smaller.
It is in the shape of a crescent now.

Day 16

The sun is shining on the side of the moon we cannot see, so it is very dark outside. Without light, I cannot see the trees!

Day 18

Tonight I can only see a little sliver of the moon in the sky. It looks like the moon is growing!

Day 21

I can see even more of the moon tonight. One half of it is visible in the sky. The sky is brighter than the last time I wrote.

Day 24

The moon is almost a big, bright ball again. Much of the moon is showing in the sky. It will not be long until the full moon is back!

Day 29

Tonight I see the full moon in the sky. It takes about 29 days for the moon to go through all of its phases. You can see some of them in this journal!

Essential Question How can observations lead to new discoveries?

Ben's Bright Idea

by Daniel Bick
illustrated by Matthew Vimislik

On an evening in the year 1755, dark clouds moved over the city of Philadelphia.

Ben hurried home. He was glad he had his umbrella.

A boy saw Ben. "Mr. Franklin, did you invent the umbrella?" he asked.

"No, but I wish I had," Ben said. "It was such a good idea."

As Ben hurried on, lightning flashed in the sky above him. Bright light filled the street. A few seconds later, Ben heard thunder.

Lightning flashed near his neighbors' roofs. Ben worried about lightning hitting houses. He had seen that lightning could start fires.

Years ago, lightning started a big fire in Philadelphia. Many buildings burnt down, and many lives were lost.

After that fire, Ben started a group of volunteers to protect buildings in Philadelphia. They battled dangerous fires and saved lives.

Ben was a good leader, and he liked to help his community. He was also a scientist and an inventor. Many of his ideas came from studying what he saw around him.

As Ben aged, he could not actively fight fires. However, he still worried about lightning causing fires. So Ben spent a lot of time studying lightning.

He even tried a dangerous experiment to test his theory. He believed that he could cause lightning to strike a specific area with the proper equipment. It turns out he was right!

Then Ben had a bright idea!

This idea was the lightning rod. It was a metal stick attached to the top of a building. A wire from the stick went down the building and was buried in the ground.

Ben proved that lightning was attracted to the metal rod and would hit it instead of the building. The energy from the lightning followed along the wire into the ground.

That way lightning would not start a fire! The lightning rod protected buildings.

Now rain fell harder as Ben entered his front door. He rushed upstairs. Ben wanted to watch the thunderstorm from a high window.

From his window, Ben watched the lightning rods on the tops of the buildings. Lightning split the sky. But none of the buildings caught on fire. His idea had protected buildings from the lightning!

Finally, the rain ended. Ben thought again about his ideas and inventions. They had made the city and people safer from thunderstorms!

Then Ben laughed. He said to himself, "But I still wish I had invented the umbrella. That was such a good idea!"

Glossary

C

cause
the reason something happens

constant
happening all the time

continues
to keep going

D

different
not alike

E

experiment
a test in which you carefully observe events and effects to learn about something

F

finally
at the end of a period of time

I

idea
a plan, thought, or suggestion

instead
in place of

invent
to create something for the first time

L

light
the brightness produced by the sun, by fire, or by a lamp

P

phases
a part or step in a process

position
the place where a person or thing is

R

really
for a fact

S

shadow
an area of darkness created when a source of light is blocked

something
one thing or another

W

where
in what place